The Druid Way
Made Easy

The Druid Way
Made Easy

Graeme K. Talboys

BOOKS

Winchester, UK
Washington, USA

First published by O-Books, 2011
O-Books is an imprint of John Hunt Publishing Ltd., The Bothy, Deershot Lodge, Park Lane,
Ropley, Hants, SO24 0BE, UK
office1@o-books.net
www.o-books.com

For distributor details and how to order please visit the 'Ordering' section on our website.

Text copyright: Graeme K. Talboys 2010

ISBN: 978 1 84694 545 8

A CIP catalogue record for this book is available from the British Library.

Design: Lee Nash

Printed in the UK by CPI Antony Rowe
Printed in the USA by Offset Paperback Mfrs, Inc

We operate a distinctive and ethical publishing philosophy in all
areas of our business, from our global network of authors to
production and worldwide distribution.

CONTENTS

Acknowledgements

My thanks go to Julie White who took the time to read the work at draft stage; and to my wife, Barbara, who not only went through the finished work with a keen eye, but also supported every stage of the project. I must, however, claim any errors as my own.

Clas Myrddin
July 2010

For all who walk in the dappled light of the Forest.

Introduction

This book is about modern Druids; what they are, what they do, and what they believe. Most people will have heard of Druids, yet they are unlikely to know very much about them. There is a wealth of information about larger religions, but when it comes to the beliefs of smaller groups of people it is a different picture. Not only is there rarely enough information, there are also insufficient terms of reference to make study and understanding easy.

One of the problems with trying to understand Druids is that their beliefs and attitudes are not derived from a sacred text or the teachings of an individual. They have no central hierarchy and no fixed ideology. Instead, they look to the natural world with which they develop a deep material and spiritual bond.

This kind of relationship with the world is often called paganism, a name which throws up another set of problems in understanding Druids. Quite aside from the fact that some Druids are wary of identifying with paganism, it has been cast in a bad light for so long that many make false assumptions about it.

'Pagan' is often used as a pejorative to mean 'uncivilized' or 'un-Christian'. Indeed, the Abrahamic traditions (Judaism, Christianity, and Islam) tend to teach that 'pagan' is synonymous with evil or the devil. Yet pagan belief systems are wholly separate from the Abrahamic religions and in many cases pre-date them.

The word 'pagan' derives from the Latin *paganus*, meaning 'rural', 'villager' and, to city-dwelling Romans, 'yokel'. It is also related to *pagus*, meaning 'village' or 'country district'. Roman soldiers were known to use *paganus* as a derogatory term for 'civilian'. Some early Christians (who considered themselves as soldiers of Christ) used 'pagan' to refer to non-Christians, but this went out of use by the fourth century AD, re-emerging only in more recent times. From the fifth century onwards, 'pagan' seems to have been used in the modern sense of a person whose beliefs are associated with the spirit or deity of the natural world.

Paganism in its modern sense encompasses shamanistic, ecstatic, magical, polytheistic, and philosophic traditions. It tends to be nature-centred, venerates both female and male deistic principles, and considers the material and the spiritual to be inextricably linked and of equal importance. Honour, trust, responsibility, friendship, tolerance, and diversity are also key elements of its general structure.

It is based on a personal relationship with the world rather than on creeds and other affirmations of transcendent deity. Nature is taken as the visible manifestation of the transcendent, which is why a veneration of the natural world is a core expression of pagan belief. This is no crude worship of trees, stones, rivers, or hills. Rather, it is a recognition and reverencing of the divine in the material world, treating nature as sacred and using it as a model for understanding.

There are, of course, a number of other aspects of paganism that make it distinct from other traditions. Many pagans are animists; they see things as cyclical and are thus more inclined to believe in some form of reincarnation; and most practice some form of ritual or natural magic.

There are 300 million pagans in the world today. The pagan resurgence in modern Western society is, broadly speaking, a form of nature mysticism that has evolved out of a metaphysical stance very different from the prevailing materialism. Whether by coincidence or design, this 'new' metaphysic resembles that of people who were and are pagan. The impetus may be modern concerns (ecological awareness, feminism, politics, and so on) in search of a spiritual framework, but it represents a re-awakening of latent ways rather than an invention of new ones.

This revitalization has taken on a variety of forms, many

without a specific tradition. Druids are those who are drawn to a particular view of the world, one derived from that of ancestral Celts. Of course, Druids today are not what Druids were two thousand or more years ago. No Druid pretends they are. Being Druid is not an academic exercise in historical role play; it is a deeply spiritual way of life. Druids use the name as an easy way of identifying themselves with the metaphysical and spiritual stance of ancestral Celts, a people who had no name for their beliefs and who probably did not think of them as a religion in the sense we now understand.

In recognition of this, 'Druid Way' is used throughout this book in preference to 'Druidry' as the latter implies a coherent set of beliefs that go by that name. There is no such set of beliefs, nor is it a name that ancestral Celts would have recognized because Druids were a great deal more than just a priestly caste. 'Druid Way' implies a route or path as well as the method by which it is travelled.

It would not be possible to explore in full the rich and varied forest that is the Druid Way in such a short book as this. What is offered is a basic map that shows the shape of the subject and which will allow you, should you so wish, to explore further without getting lost.

Part I

1

The Celts

Understanding the Druid of today means understanding the Druid of the past and the context in which they existed – Celtic society. There continues to be a lively debate about the nature of the Celtic world, both past and present. A great deal of shoddy research, coupled with poor argument has done little to clarify things. Happily there are also many sane voices concerned with developing and extending our understanding of the Celts.

Whilst it is true that there were recognizably similar forms of burial practice, ritual behaviour, settlement layouts, distinctive art styles, a group of closely related languages, common mythical themes, and similar social structures across a wide geographical area, this does not mean the Celts were a homogeneous group. There were wide variations through time as the culture evolved in response to internal and external pressures. There were also wide variations from place to place. It is the language and common cultural practices that bound these peoples together.

Archaeological evidence currently dates the earliest phase of Celtic culture to around 1200 BC, well back into the Bronze Age. The Bronze Age as a whole was one of increasing settlement and improved agriculture. By 1500 BC, there is evidence of successful mixed farming, crop rotation, and a pattern of social complexity. The Indo-European language was beginning to fragment into distinct types and an early form of Celtic was probably being spoken.

Celtic culture is divided into two major periods. The earlier of these is called the Hallstatt (named for the village in Austria where archaeological evidence was first found). The Hallstatt itself has four phases. A and B correspond with the Late Bronze Age. With the introduction of iron, we see the beginning of phase C, a comparatively short period of enormous change. Hallstatt D, which was also comparatively short, marks a shift westward of the Celtic heartland to the Rhône, the Loire, and the headwaters of the Seine.

The mainstay of the Celtic economy was farming. The introduction of iron tools allowed for greater productivity and increased wealth. Prosperity and leisure occasioned a growth in population and trade. By the time that Hallstatt Celts were well established in the area we now call Austria, Celtic culture had spread into most of Western Europe, including the south-eastern corner of Britain.

There was a marked change across Europe in the middle of the fifth century BC. Constant warfare in the eastern Mediterranean disrupted trade links and caused a shift in power in Celtic lands. In a relatively short period of time, Hallstatt gave way to the second major period of Celtic culture – the La Tène (after the site in Switzerland where archaeological evidence was first uncovered).

There was a distinct change in social structure. Hallstatt Celts buried their elite in rustic wagons with other grave goods. Any weapons were largely those used for hunting or for ceremonial display; an indication that farmers and traders were also chieftains. La Tène Celts buried their elite with two-wheeled chariots and weapons of war. The leaders of society were now warriors.

The La Tène period was more turbulent, and at such times warrior elites come to the fore. They take the risks on behalf of others in their tribe and they reap the rewards.

La Tène influence was vigorous. By the third and second centuries BC, it was to be found in what we now know as Ireland, Britain, northern and western Spain, virtually the whole of France, northern Italy, Switzerland, Belgium, the Netherlands, western Germany, the Czech and Slovak Republics, Romania,

Bulgaria, and the Republics of the former Yugoslavia as far south as the northern borders of Macedonia. Celtic peoples even colonized a large part of central Turkey, which became known as Galatia. Moreover, they traded well beyond these areas and played an important role in the histories of other peoples.

In 295 BC, the Romans began their own long expansion. It was no walkover. When Caesar was assassinated in 44 BC, Gaul was still not wholly under Roman control and the much-vaunted invasion of Britain had been little more than a flag-waving exercise.

Throughout central Europe, trade with and occupation by Rome increasingly diluted Celtic culture. The last remaining strongholds of the La Tène, and the places where it had its greatest flowering, were Britain and Ireland.

It is during the period of the Roman occupation of Western Europe that most accounts of the Celts come to an end, as if they had somehow faded away. Yet Celtic peoples continued to live and work as they always had. Whilst they were driven westward over the centuries by waves of invaders and settlers, this pressure failed to destroy Celtic culture. Celtic peoples and their distinctive languages and view of the world still exist and are now enjoying something of a revival.

Most of what we know of the social structure of the Celts relates to the late Iron Age. Law texts and literature (some not written down until the twelfth or thirteenth century AD although clearly of much earlier origin) are our best sources for this. Although they are open to interpretation, they are the best evidence we have and a great deal of work has gone into understanding what they mean and what they might imply.

Celtic society was agricultural. Whilst settlements large enough to be called towns existed, the most common unit of settlement would have been the farmstead. These ranged in size from single family holdings to clusters that we would now call villages.

It is no surprise, therefore, that most people worked on the land and at trades allied to that and to supplying domestic needs. Farmers and artisans were the core and the bulk of society. They supplied a sufficient surplus not only to trade, but also to support two other sections of society who were non-productive but nonetheless important to a complex social structure.

The first of these is usually referred to as the warrior class. This is slightly misleading. There is a general perception of Celts as a warlike people, always fighting. The truth is they were far less militaristic than other contemporaneous cultures. That did not mean they could not fight or that they had no professional warriors. Indeed, their warriors were renowned and feared, as was the fact the whole population (including women) would come armed to the battlefield. However, they did not have large standing armies. Tribal chiefs and regional rulers had bodyguards, but these would be relatively small groups and would have spent most of their time acting as border guards and policemen.

The other class of society – the doctors, teachers, judges, advisers, historians, lawyers, diplomats, scientists, and priests – were known collectively as Druids. Perhaps because of the modern emphasis on spiritual matters, and certainly because of the fantasies of eighteenth century antiquarians, Druids are commonly thought of as having been wizardly priests. Some were, perhaps. But they fulfilled all the other roles required by a complex society not met by makers and protectors.

However, Druids were more than a mere collection of various professionals. Celtic society had levels of social mobility, equality, and justice still only dreamed of in large parts of the world today. But it was a tribal culture and most people did not travel great distances. Druids, because of their training, the high esteem in which they were held, their knowledge, and their mobility, bound Celtic society more tightly than would otherwise have been the case. They were also a network through which communication could be achieved, even between tribes historically hostile. It was for this that the Romans considered them a threat.

Some sense in which Druids were more than the sum of their parts can be found in the meaning of 'druid'. The word *Druidae* first began to appear in the second century BC. There had been earlier references to *sacerdotes, antistites, gutuartos,* and the like, but it was not until the Greek Poseidonius (c.135-c.50 BC) travelled through Gaul that there was a realization that all intellectual functionaries in Celtic society were known collectively as Druids.

Speculation on the origin and meaning of the word began at an early date. Pliny the Elder thought it possible that *druid* was taken from the Greek word *drus,* which means 'oak'. Lucan refers to them as *dryadae,* which may be an attempt to link them with Greek wood spirits. Other forms also appear, including *drasidae* and *drysidae*. The connection with trees was strong from the earliest period.

Although words from one language are adopted into another, it is highly unlikely that a well-established and integral institution of Celtic society would have been known by anything other than a native name. The Greek word *druidai* and the Latin *druidae* and *druides* are consistent with a Celtic form **druvis,* from **druvids*. As this word does not appear in any known Romano-Celtic inscription, its existence can only remain conjectural, but it is consistent with known words.

Both elements of the word *druvis* (*dru* and *wid*) are widely accepted Celtic and Indo-European root words. Most authorities agree that *wid* means 'to know' or 'to see' which encompass the whole idea of understanding, of great importance to a class of society responsible for all aspects of the intellect.

But what is it that is seen or known? Celtic languages all have similar words for 'oak'. The Gallic is *dervo*. Other early forms are *daur* (Gaelic), *derw* (Welsh), and *derv* (Breton). Modern versions are similar in form – *dair* (Irish), *darach* (Gaelic), *daragh* (Manx), *derwen* and *dâr* (Welsh), *derowen* (Cornish), and *dervenn* (Breton). It is entirely possible that they derive from a common Indo-European root **deru*.

If this is correct and *dru* can be taken to mean 'oak', then *druid* would mean something like 'one who sees or knows the oak', perhaps more comfortably rendered as 'oak-seer' or 'oak-knower'. This is not entirely beyond the realms of plausibility, especially if we accept a long development of the class, starting in a time when hunter-gatherers were still prevalent. Those who had knowledge of the oak (and, by extension, the forests) would have played an important role in society.

Dru has also been interpreted as *dreo*, meaning 'truth'. Given that the root of both words is probably the same and that truth is a central tenet of ancestral Celtic thought and belief, there is a strong degree of plausibility in this interpretation. A Druid as one who sees and knows the truth certainly reflects accurately the function of Druids in society.

Druids may originally have been knowers of the oak, but the meaning broadened as the role of the oak-knower increased in complexity. The wise men and women of the proto-Celtic peoples may have been shamanistic in nature, guiding their people through the forests of this world and the spirit world. With the settled existence brought about by the introduction of farming, the role of the oak-knowers would have had to change or fade away.

By the Iron Age, 'oak-knowers' had evolved into 'truth-knowers'. Yet although their role became more complex, their core function did not. Knowing the forest and being able to guide their people would have meant knowing the truth of all things. This fundamental aspect remained at the same time as its application adapted in response to a changing social environment.

2

The Celtic Metaphysic

We know *how* Celts behaved, but it is equally important to know *why* they behaved as they did. It goes without saying that reconstructing the way a people thinks is fraught with difficulty. Yet just as we can accurately surmise the optimal shape of the foundation of a building by studying its structure, so we can reconstruct the likely metaphysic of a culture by studying that culture's shape and how it has changed in response to pressure.

There are three main sources for reconstruction, supplemented by the historical and archaeological record. The first of these are the myths, wonder tales, poetry, and folklore of the Celtic people, which are sometimes collectively known as the Matter of Ireland and the Matter of Britain. Second is the collection of non-fictional writings that have come down to us, principally the law texts from both Ireland and Wales. Finally there is the language of the Celts. Even today, when Celtic languages have been subject to alteration from outside pressures, word use, syntax, grammar, and vocabulary all provide clues as to how the Celts thought about the world and dealt with ethical matters.

This still leaves a number of considerations. Reconstruction and discussion of the metaphysic must be done with reference to the metaphysic of our own culture. Our way of looking at the world is so deeply ingrained we have trouble accepting that there might be other ways of doing so. This is largely because the means by which we learn about the world (as well as the content of what we learn) are determined by the precepts of that metaphysic. Each reinforces the other.

Notwithstanding this, it is possible to study a culture and

tease out something of the basic patterns that underlie the way in which its peoples behaved as they did. It is important to remember, however, that what follows is simply a description of some strands of metaphysical thought that have been deduced from the available sources. It is neither complete nor organized, other than for the ease of readers. Indeed, too rigid a system of thought would have been counter to the metaphysic with which Celts were raised.

Celts viewed the world as synthetic, organicistic, and holistic. This was the basis of everything else as their concern was with understanding the real world, their place within it, and the inter-connectedness of all things. Many of the laws that have come down to us are concerned with relationships. Many of the tales and myths explore the consequences of broken relationships. And these are relationships at all levels, between people, animals, plants, the wider world, and the deities of the Celtic pantheon.

Synthetic

Synthesis means to combine distinct things and concepts to form a complex whole. It is about knowing the world; about making, building, and growth. And not simply in physical or material terms, but spiritual as well. It is a recognition of the fact that, whilst things might be distinct one from another, they are not actually separate.

Synthesis is also about natural processes and learning to work with them. This was considered an essential of physical and spiritual evolution. In specific terms, we can see this at work in the idea that the spiritual side of life is as important as, and inextricably linked with, the material side. A person was not considered complete if both aspects were not treated equally. That is why exile from clan or tribe was the ultimate punishment as it divorced a person from both material *and* spiritual connection and sustenance.

Organicistic

Organicism means that the parts of a whole can only be understood properly in relation to their functions within the complex and evolving whole; with the whole envisioned as a living entity. Thus, a meadow flower can only be properly understood in relation to its function in any given whole to which it belongs, be that a meadow, a food web, the life cycle of an insect, the inspiration of a poet, and so on. The same is true with people. Their behaviour can only be understood in relation to all the people about them, the structure of the society in which they live, and their natural environment. There is also an awareness that an ill-considered action may lead, through complex networks, to quite unforeseen and disastrous consequences. This notion is quite often the theme of the myths and legends of the Celtic peoples.

Holistic

Holistic means that in terms of systems and living things, the whole is greater than the sum of its parts. Evidence of this attitude can be found in the relationship of the person to the tribe. The tribe itself was considered a living entity that had its own sentience, its own behaviour, and its own relationships. The tribe cared for the individual (there is plenty of evidence of highly advanced forms of social welfare) and, in return, the individual cared for the tribe.

Celts did not spend their time seeing how they could apply these concepts to their world. It was simply how they understood the world to be. There may well, however, have been some Druids who explored these ideas, for we know that Druids were accounted great philosophers and theologians. Their role as a cohesive force in society would certainly suggest that they had some understanding, not just of the main structure of their metaphysic, but of the more specific aspects discussed below.

Concordant

The concept of unity was a strong and overarching element of the Celtic metaphysic. All things, all aspects of being, were connected. They probably believed that the distinctions between discrete objects were due to particular attributes of a single underlying essence, much as the facets of a crystal. This would certainly accommodate the notion of shape shifting and of the movement of the soul from one world to the next. It would also account for other aspects of a generally concordant view – that balance, harmony, and order are essential elements not just of society but also of the world as a whole.

Cyclical

As an agricultural people, Celts would have been highly conscious of the cyclical patterns of life. Circadian and lunar rhythms provided basic timekeeping. Crops and livestock would be born, grow, flourish, and die. The seasons would turn. Every nineteen years the lunar and solar cycles would coincide.

The concept of the cyclical was not confined to the material world. The spiritual journey of the Celts was also seen in cyclic terms with death leading to rebirth in the Otherworld, where the next cycle was played out before the soul returned to this world.

Furthermore, there was an understanding from the example of nature that things move on. No seed produces an exact replica of the plant that formed it, just as no child is an exact replica of its parents. Lessons are learned and carried forward; all aspects of life evolve or wither away.

Realistic

Celts were firmly attached to reality. Their whole lives were lived in intimate relationship with the world about them. They faced the realities of everyday life without hiding them away or letting someone else deal with them.

This realism can be regarded as a form of naturalism, with no distinction made between the natural and the supernatural. Rather, there was a distinction made between what they could and could not understand. Deities and magical events were part of the natural order.

Magical

Celts had an excellent grasp of science and technology. You do not carry out successful brain surgery, smelt iron, create exquisite enamels, or construct complex stone buildings to heights of thirty feet or more without it. Their lives and their thinking, however, were not governed by a scientific paradigm. Rather, they saw the world as magical.

We should not be confused by this term into thinking of some vague and superstitious nonsense. Magic is a study of the underlying principles of something and working with those principles to effect some end. Some would argue that this is science and technology. These, however, are concerned only with the material and there is much more to the world than that.

To study and perform magically requires a different view of what constitutes knowledge, as well as of its ultimate value. Whilst recognizing that knowledge had intrinsic worth (in that it was a condition of human existence), Celts were not interested in it for its own sake. It was there to be used for a better understanding of the material and non-material world.

Veritable

Druids (at least, those who were philosophers) were much concerned with understanding the nature of the universe and the place of humanity within it. Judging by Old Irish texts, the central concept of this search was that of truth. Although we cannot assume that the preoccupations of Irish Druid philosophers were shared universally, it does seem that the concept of truth is so basic to an understanding of the world that it was common to all Celts.

Truth was considered to be important to much more than just human affairs. It meant much more than veracity of language. In fact, truth was regarded by Celts as the sustaining power of all creation. In the myths, an act of truth (be that by word, thought, or deed) was endowed with power.

The Druid Morann mac Cairbre (in his will) stated that 'through the ruler's truth all the land is fruitful and every child born worthy'. Other references to truth in the same text refer to its power to avert disaster, bring tranquillity, increase knowledge, and preserve life.

Since truth is the controlling principle of the universe, it follows that whatever happens in the universe, happens in accord with truth. The natural world is a place of truth. The only exception can be through the exercise of free will.

Being untruthful has a cost. In Celtic myth, this usually results in the person who commits a false act being blemished with spots or an illness. The consequences, however, can be far more severe. If, as suggested by Morann mac Cairbre, truth makes the land fruitful, then the opposite must also be the case. Rulers who have responsibility for the land and their people can bring disaster and famine if they are untruthful or allow deceit to flourish. The whole of the Grail cycle of tales (despite its later Christian embroidery) is predicated on this basic idea.

Ethical

Honour and responsibility are mentioned repeatedly in Celtic literature, and Celts were no doubt imbued with these concepts from an early age. Of course, one can only be truly responsible if one has freedom of action and of will. It is true that certain obligations were placed on members of society, and these constrained them in some ways, but on the whole, Celtic society was free and highly egalitarian – even by today's standards. We know that the concept of free will figured strongly in the Celtic metaphysic. Not only is it apparent in literature, where tales often hang on the choice made by individuals, but it also played a large part in what is known as the Pelagian 'heresy'. The 'British heresy', as it was also known, was regarded by the Christian Church of the fifth century as Druidic philosophy which had to be repressed.

Freedom is not absolute; it is freedom, not license, and must be balanced by attendant responsibilities. Living in a close-knit tribal society would demonstrate that the freedom to do things and to make whatever choices one wishes is relative to everyone else's freedom. Decisions and actions all have an effect on others and on the environment that sustains them.

Honour (that is, a sense of justice) derives in part from seeing the world as unified, of seeing that balance and harmony are essential. This quite naturally extends to human relationships with the wider world. Celts, however, recognized that people are shaped largely by their relationship with other people. A society in which everyone treats everyone else in a just fashion is not only easier to live in, but it is one that requires far fewer rigid rules and methods of enforcement.

Responsibility was also very personal. Each person was responsible for their own thoughts and deeds. What is more, the legal system ensured that people were responsible for repairing any damage they caused. This was standardized by the setting of an honour price for transgressions. This could be paid in money or by working off the debt.

Dynamic

Life is innately creative. It constantly engages with the world to make it favourable for itself. The Celts knew this and saw creation itself as ongoing. This vigour is an essential of Celtic life and not just in simplistic terms of physical vigour. Their whole culture (physical, mental, and spiritual) was bursting at the seams with life.

A consequence of this positive attitude to life was that Celts were extremely assertive and would defend themselves fiercely.

They felt no need to justify or apologize for their existence.

In tandem with this vigour was a recognition of the essential balancing factor – quiescence. The two went together as naturally as waking and sleeping, summer and winter, day and night. One without the other is unhealthy and unsustainable. Quiescence itself can have a dynamic aspect in that it is a life-enhancing state. It also means knowing when to stop, which is not the same thing as knowing how far you can go. It speaks of an acute awareness of a world beyond the ego and the need to lead a balanced life.

Personalist

Personalism deems the person to be the starting point of an understanding of the world. This is not to place the person at the centre of the universe and make all other things subordinate. It merely points out that as it is the person who does the understanding, it is the person that is the reference point for that understanding (rather than *a priori* truths or empirical scientific facts).

Precisely what constitutes a person has long been a matter of debate. On two things, however, Personalists and Celts are agreed. The first is that the fundamental structure of the person is both matter and spirit. The second is that the person is not an atomistic individual, but a being whose nature is formed by and implies community.

This view made for strong social cohesion. When people are formed by community and derive part of their identity from it, their needs and the needs of their social group (be it family, clan, or tribe) are rarely at odds. What is good for the person is good for the group. What is good for both is good for the place in which they live, for this too was part of the community and also contributed to the identity of person.

This was never a denial of the person. The community was not the whole of a person's identity, just the fertile soil in which each person could flourish. The wellbeing of the person was the starting point of all endeavours and the final measure of success.

Economics, politics, philosophy, agriculture, art, science, religion, education, technology... all began with the communal and ecological existence of the person and were used to satisfy their needs by doing the most with the least. All of these things, attached to the reality of human life in and of the world, were vastly enriched and enriching through the personalist approach to existence.

Sacred

Celts were well aware that we each have an inner life. They did not regard this as something that made us separate, either one from another or from the rest of the world. Rather, it was what joined each with the others, all with the world, and all with the ineffable.

Being aware of this communion was important. Celts felt a direct link with the sacred, not because they regarded themselves as a chosen people but because they knew they were an integral part of the world. They were connected because all things were connected.

Celtic culture reflects the idea that the universe is ensouled and therefore sacred. There may have been differences in emphasis, but Celts lived in a sacred environment, their whole lives being an act of communion with spirit and with deity. And true to the way in which they viewed the world, their perspective was very personal. The sacred was in the everyday, in the tasks of ordinary life, in relationships with other people and the land. This was reflected even in their great religious festivals, with the everyday transactions of the market place and personal relationships being given special force at these times of year. Yet the high days and holy days marked the public face of their belief. At the personal level, they believed that if they acted honourably and responsibly in the everyday things, the cycles of their lives would eventually bring them to an understanding of the greater things that were currently beyond their comprehension.

3

Survival and Revival

Is it possible that ancestral Celtic beliefs and philosophy have survived through the last two millennia? Academics are certainly divided on the question. Most people, if they think about it at all, assume that such things would have died when the Druids were destroyed by the Romans.

The only problem is that the Romans did not destroy the Druids or even contemplate such a task. That would have meant destroying the entire intellectual class of the Celtic peoples – teachers, doctors, engineers, historians, priests, and so on. Such a campaign, if it had taken place, would have been mentioned somewhere in the historical record, especially if it had been successful. Furthermore, the Roman Empire did not extend as far as Ireland or have much influence in the western and northern fringes of Britain.

When Rome formally withdrew its protection of Britain in AD 410, the structure of Celtic society was largely intact – including the presence of the Druids. This meant that the schools still existed, which, in turn, meant that both the Celtic metaphysic and Celtic beliefs and religious practices also still existed.

From the fourth century onwards, Christianity grew in strength and influence. Nor was it backward in spreading the good word. Martin of Tours, for example, set about converting the people of Gaul, leading a mob that destroyed pagan groves and shrines wherever they found them, as well as attacking Druids who even at that early stage were being regarded solely as priests and keepers of the old ways.

Quite when Christianity reached Britain and Ireland is not known. Distinctly Christian buildings appear in the archaeological record in the late third century AD, suggesting a settled Christian presence perhaps as early as the middle of the second century. Yet paganism still seems to have been the norm in the fifth century, despite some historians suggesting that Christianity was widespread and firmly rooted. This was not just Celtic paganism, but Saxon and Norse as well. When Germanus visited Britain in AD 429, it was to dispose of the Pelagian heresy, which was considered a threat to the Church. What he discovered was that many Britons still adhered to their pagan religion and were officially sanctioned in this by chieftains and kings.

In Ireland, a real and lasting effort was made to accommodate both paganism and Christianity. In AD 438, High King Lóegaire mac Néill appointed a commission of nine eminent persons to study, revise, and commit to writing the laws of Ireland. The nine were comprised of three *breitheamh* (Brehon), three Christians, and three kings. The resultant law code, based firmly in Celtic culture and preserving the concepts of responsibility and honour rather than that of retribution, survived until the mid-seventeenth century.

In the mid-sixth century, Kentigern found that paganism was strong in the south of Strathclyde, taught by Bards and officially recognized. The Battle of Arderydd (AD 573), at which Myrddin is said to have gone mad at the sight of so much slaughter, was fought between Christian and pagan kingdoms. Whether or not this was a religious dispute is not known, but it does demonstrate that paganism still existed in the late sixth century.

At the same time, the High King of Ireland was inviting Gildas and other monks to travel to his lands to help revive Christianity, which was falling out of favour. This was largely because of its antagonistic stance over matters of doctrine, which the Church claimed should apply universally rather than just to Christians. On the Continent, the Third Council of Toledo had declared against the sacrilegious idolatry that was firmly rooted and widespread throughout Iberia and Gaul. All of which sounds very much as if pagans were still using their shrines and sacred places for worship, despite Christian attempts to destroy them.

Where they could not be suppressed, many pagan ideas and practices were absorbed wholesale into Christianity. Major solar festivals were incorporated into Church usage and lost their uniquely Celtic character and name. Pagan gods and goddesses were either condemned as demons and devils or converted hastily into local saints. Doctrine and theology were also subsumed.

Although officially sanctioned Celtic paganism began to fade, it still flourished unofficially. And alongside it, a distinct form of Christianity evolved as the official religion. These days, to refer to Celtic Christianity is to draw down the wrath of sections of the academic community, but it cannot be denied that Rome considered the British Church (as they called it) not only to be distinct but also seriously 'infected' by Druidic philosophy.

When the priestly function was forbidden to any but Christians, and the Druid schools were outlawed, Druids continued to exist. Nor did the Druid schools disappear. With the simple expediency of calling themselves Bardic schools and with judicious minor alterations to their syllabuses, they continued much as before.

Even though dispersed and their schools officially closed, Druids survived and helped keep alive the Celtic metaphysic. In the tenth century AD, and possibly later, the Kings of Cashel in Ireland were still being gifted Druids. Welsh Bards in the twelfth century AD wrote openly of the Druids who still lived, practiced, and taught in their country. Gerald of Wales mentions the existence of Vates or soothsayers, giving a vivid description of their methods as well as offering scriptural support for what they did and how they did it.

Even so, much was being lost and would have faded altogether were it not for an enthusiasm by monastic communities for writing down all they could of native lore. The birth of

Celtic nationalism ensured that some, at least, of the ancient tales and poems were recorded. Although many of the texts have Christian additions and glosses, they retain their pagan character.

From the seventh to the eleventh centuries, the poems by and attributed to Aneirin, Myrddin, and Taliesin were set down, as were the tales we now know as *The Mabinogion*. Most of the great Irish epics were also written down during this period. All these texts contain densely packed and multi-layered tales, which suggests that they are of great antiquity.

Whilst this aspect of the past was being preserved, pagan practices continued. The church in Dingwall, near Inverness, makes report in 1656 of bulls being sacrificed to St Mourie – a thinly disguised *Mór Rí*, which translates as 'Great King'. These rites were attended by locals, by strangers (that is, Scots from other parts of the country), and by visitors from foreign countries. Clearly something more than a local folk custom is taking place here.

A century later, in 1774, there are still reports of people in the Highlands honouring places associated with *Mór Rí* by leaving small gifts. That would suggest mere folk custom were it not also for the fact that that we have reports of a pagan priesthood still in operation toward the end of the eighteenth century. On the island of Maelrubha in Loch Maree (*Mór Rí*?), which is in Wester Ross, there was a sacred oak attended by priests, along with a well said to have healing properties. Sacred wells and trees were not uncommon, but that there were priests who tended them and officiated at rites speaks of some level of organization and the transmission of knowledge, even if it was by that time restricted to a particular clan or family.

In Ireland and Scotland, the Bardic schools survived as formal institutions until the early eighteenth century, and would have helped to sustain elements of both metaphysic and pagan belief by providing an authoritative source for genealogy, history, and myth. The changing political scene saw the patronage of these schools destroyed. Yet even then, into the late eighteenth century there were clansmen in the Highlands and Islands of Scotland who were sending their sons to be trained as Bards. To be sure, these were not Druids, but the link with the past was still strong and these Bards fulfilled many of the functions of their Druid forebears.

All this survived, despite the many attempts that had been made to suppress paganism and impose a Christian orthodoxy on the people. Celtic and (latterly) Saxon pagan practices and beliefs were simply too deeply ingrained. Even the Protestant Reformation, which made a deliberate and concerted effort to stamp out pagan practice, did little to change the way in which people thought and acted in their everyday lives. The period of the Long Parliament in England and Wales (1642-1653) saw a systematic effort to destroy folk customs, especially May Day celebrations, which had a particular association with fertility. Although maypoles may have disappeared in large numbers, the people simply learned to make their devotions more discretely or in private.

The eighteenth century saw a new element to this tale. Partly as a backlash against the austerities of Puritanism, but also because of a growing interest in British heritage, antiquaries turned their eyes away from Classical studies and began to look much closer to home. Even today in the Western world, Greek and Roman culture and languages are considered in some way superior to all others. Most people in Celtic countries will know more about Classical history, myth, and institutions than those of their native lands. In the eighteenth century, the first steps in redressing the balance were taken.

With more enthusiasm than accuracy to begin with, large numbers of scholarly gentlemen began to expound on the Druids, their practices, dress, origins, and their teachings. The paganism associated with the native peoples of the Celtic lands was seen as acceptable, no doubt because of the efforts of these

27

scholars (many of whom were Christian clerics) to link Celtic paganism with the religion of the Jewish patriarchs and, by association, with Christianity.

The integrity and veracity of the work of these Druid revivalists has long since been called into question and found severely wanting. It cannot, however, be dismissed out of hand. To begin with, there was a genuine belief held by these men that they were reviving a living tradition, part of which was Bardism. They were educated people and a few were truly inspired poets and visionaries. Some muddied the academic pool by inventing what did not exist and by 'adapting' what did, but we can condemn them no more than we can condemn the early hagiographers of Christian tradition.

Although these scholars may have failed to attain standards we now find acceptable, they did manage to make three important contributions. The first was that they made Celtic studies acceptable to people who had previously dismissed Celts both past and present as mere barbarians. Secondly, they made paganism acceptable and helped to keep it alive at a time when traditional practices in the countryside were fading away.

Their third achievement is more tenuous, but perhaps the most important. Whilst the accuracy of their facts and the strength of their arguments are now open to question, they did much to keep alive the Celtic metaphysic. This was an indirect consequence of their work, but at a time when scientific materialism was growing in strength and influence, these eccentrics and pseudo-scholars kept alive the idea that there are many ways of looking at and understanding the world.

That the Revivalists had a great impact on modern Druidry is without question. That their influence has been superseded is also without question. Even as they were making their studies and forming the first Druid Orders, compiling their books and discussing the finer points of sacred geometry, the other strand of pagan survival was continuing unobtrusively. After all, being

Druid (in any age) has little to do with book learning. It is a way of conducting the self in accord with a particular way of viewing the world.

Tracing the survival of the Celtic metaphysic from the late seventeenth century to the present day is not easy, but we do catch glimpses of its existence if we know where to look. In that search, it is important to remember that this was not a conscious dispersal of ideas. Rather it was a reaction of ordinary folk to changes that a minority of society attempted to impose on them. They may have paid lip service to new ways and ideas (those that filtered out from the centres of so-called civilization), but they stuck with those that they knew would work.

This does not mean that Druid teachings, the rites and beliefs of Celtic paganism, or the Celtic metaphysic have come down to us intact. Far from it. However, the same is true for all religions. The world changes, things get lost, others get changed, new ideas flower. Yet sufficient has survived to mark the long path over the centuries, enabling Druids today to remain in touch with their roots whilst also living in the world of the twenty-first century.

Part II

4

The Inner World

The metaphysic of modern Druids is derived from sources held in common with ancestral Celts as well as from writings that were made from the beginnings of the historical period. It is from this fertile ground that the doctrine of modern Druids is gleaned. Yet it is clear that this is not doctrine as most religions would understand it.

When people become Druid, it is usually out of a realization that they have already developed a view of the world that is akin to the Celtic metaphysic and are living their lives in accord with it. All they lack is a formal framework through which this can be expressed.

Not everyone in this situation is attracted by the pagan Celtic view of the world; not all those who do follow a Celtic path call themselves Druid. The important point is that they have already chosen to live by certain codes of behaviour. No one can be forced to adopt the Celt metaphysic; that would be to violate its basic precepts. It is why Druids do not try to convert others and it is why they are reluctant to undertake formal teaching of the Way to anyone under the age of eighteen. They consider such things to be unethical.

As with the metaphysic, it is possible to tease out some of the tenets by which Druids live their lives. Although individual threads are interesting, it should be remembered that the way they are woven together is equally important. The warp of this cloth is truth.

Truth

Truth as a concept is all too often connected solely with

language. Yet it is much broader than that. Indeed, Truth has to expand from a narrow notion of the verity of language to one that applies to the rightness or fitness of all things, in whatever form they exist or are made manifest. This applies to spoken and written statements, certainly, but it also includes actions, constructs, thoughts, emotions, places, and ideas. Notions of falsehood must then take their shape from this.

Underlying the universe are patterns and relationships that constitute what some call the natural order and others call the laws of nature. Understanding and working in concord with those patterns and relationships to achieve some particular right end is what Druids do. This is also sometimes known as magic.

If we were to make a distinction, it would be that magic is the right working with that principle whilst truth is the right measure of that principle. That is, magic is understanding the rightness or fitness of a word, of an action, of behaviour, of the way we live, and using that understanding to achieve some right desired end. Truth is the degree to which the word, the action, the behaviour, the way we live is in accord with the underlying patterns of the universe.

This means little without defining the term 'nature'. It cannot be used to mean 'the world as it would be if untainted by outside influence' because the world is, by definition, everything. Nor can it be put in opposition to something we might call human activity because no matter how harsh that activity might be, it is the product of a species that is part of nature.

What is required is a borderline somewhere within the field of human activity, one that runs between those things we do by instinct and those over which we exercise free will. This interface is fluid and complex.

Ancestral Druids understood this. Being aware of and under-standing this is a task faced by Druids today as well, but in a world more complicated than our ancestors could have imagined. Which means that those who follow the Druid Way must know and understand the universe and the patterns and relationships on which it is based as well as the way in which it evolves. This is the Truth that Druids seek.

Service

Truth provides the raw material with which Druids work. They believe they must use the knowledge and the understanding they have. Indeed, knowledge and understanding are quite meaningless unless they *are* applied. The work they do as Druids is known as service. Truth and service are inextricably linked. For ancestral Druids, service was ultimately concerned with maintaining balance – materially, socially, and spiritually. Today, it about restoring the balance that once existed – it is about showing that there are boundaries, showing that the universe has a voice that must be heard, showing that there are better paths to tread.

Seeking out the truth, be it reaching for the absolute or working with particular instances, enables the Druid to right action. Right action has two essential elements. The first is that it must be in concord with natural law. The means to an end must be in harmony with the end, otherwise the enterprise fails before it begins. The other is that the end must not be personal. Right action might benefit those who undertake it, but that must not be the goal – otherwise it is not right action. If you grow vegetables organically, you should do it because it is in concord with the universe and beneficial to wildlife. You still get tasty and wholesome vegetables. The difference is that the means by which you achieve that end are in harmony with natural law and increase the degree to which unity is achieved.

Honour and responsibility

Although Druids have no single definitive moral code handed to them by a deity or a prophet, they do have a highly developed sense of ethics. Because the rules are not available in a handy little book, they have to work all the time to ensure that what they think, say, and do are ethical and relevant. Their adherence to the central importance of truth, combined with their belief in freedom of will, leads them to practice a form of Situation Ethics. That is, their ethical stance is based on certain precepts, but is also dependent upon the circumstances of a given situation.

Social structures, ethical considerations, and the judicial system were very different two thousand and more years ago in the Celtic world. Yet the basis on which Druids approached ethical questions is still workable and relevant today, even in a world dominated by a metaphysic from which are derived strict and complicated legal and ethical systems that are backed up with the threat of retributive punishment for those who transgress.

The trouble with a system like that, a Druid would contend, is that it exists outwith the person. There is no sense of inherency, no sense of engagement. In particular, responsibility is perceived as lying elsewhere. Society is so complicated and disjointed, so highly competitive and adversarial, that it is easy to feel that laws and ethical systems are lacking in relevance to everyday life. Law-makers, enforcers (a term that says a great deal in itself), judges, and moralists are rarely part of the community they are meant to serve.

Honour, if it is to flourish, requires an intelligent and free response to life in general and to all specific situations. Freedom of will is crucial. If someone has no genuine choice, then no matter how well that person may seem to behave, it has not been done honourably. It is the same with responsibility. Where one acts from freedom of will, one has to be prepared to accept responsibility for what one has done. No one and nothing else can be blamed. The two, honour and responsibility, are inextricably linked, part of a cycle. To take responsibility (in any sense of the word) is to behave honourably. To behave honourably is to take responsibility for one's place in the world.

Respect

Many Druids live unconventionally and their metaphysical stance often places them at the edge of or completely 'outside' of the society in which they live. This can make life difficult, but Druids do not consider themselves beyond or superior to society. They are respectful of the ways of others, even if they do not always like them.

This does not mean that Druids are acquiescent. Where there are points of conflict, they work to resolve these issues. If there are aspects of society they feel to be wrong, they work to change them. However, they will do so in a way that is in accord with their principles.

Respect is not confined to the human realm. Druids believe that the world and everything in it is endowed with spirit. This does not mean that the world should not be touched. What it does mean is that Druids recognize an essential unity of life. Believing that all things are connected, they identify with the rest of the world. That means they take care to live there as lightly as they can.

For some this means embracing vegetarianism or becoming vegan. Those that do not, take care about the sources of their food, eschewing anything produced by factory farming and artificial genetic modification. They are generally well informed on these and other issues and are often actively involved in work to protect animals from cruelty, forests from destruction, the Land and the Sea from wholesale devastation, the displacement of indigenous peoples by large corporations, and so on.

Unity and identity

Celtic poems, often ascribed to Bards, display a deep affinity with the rest of creation. Whereas most people might consider or express their connection with the natural world by analogy, Druids believe they are identical. This stems from the distinction that Druids learn to make between what is our self and what is not our self.

Whilst genetics sets up some of the parameters within which we are and can be influenced, who we are is the result of all the environments in which we circulate. Within those environments, the single largest influential factor is other people and we evolve as persons by interacting with them. We all do this in different ways and to different degrees but it is people who make people.

Whilst important to recognize, Druids contend that this is often to the neglect of other elements of the many environments in which we exist. Even with no people around, we constantly interact with our environment. And that, too, constitutes a series of relationships.

If this is so, where does each person stop and the rest of the world begin? This is not a spurious question. It is fundamental to the way in which we treat the planet. If we answer that, as persons, we stop at the epidermis and the rest of the world starts from there, Druids believe we alienate ourselves from everything else that exists and cannot truly claim to know anything about the world with any certainty. The world becomes other, unknowable, and untouchable. Thus isolated, our vision of ourselves becomes synchronous and synonymous with our body. That becomes our central concern. We become truly selfish.

There is another position, one that is adopted by pagans in general and Druids in particular. That position is that we interact with the world and that what we are is due (if only in part) to that interaction. Therefore, as persons, we do not stop at the epidermis, but extend beyond that to include all that we experience at any given time. This will include other people, animals, plants, objects, machines, ideas, sensations, dreams, and so on.

If during normal, everyday life, our being enfolds all that we interact with and experience, then we are inseparable from the world. We go through life expanding and contracting in a vital dance in which the essential self lives its own life without ever being separated from creation. We are all part of one another, part of every creature, part of all that is.

If this is so, then if we harm any part of the world, a Druid would contend, we also harm ourselves. We cannot avoid changing the world as we pass through; that is a function of living. We can recognize, however, that we are a part of it and a part of other people as much as it and they are part of us. Our passage through the world should be a gentle one – if only to minimize harm to our self. Do this and we become, not selfish, but self-interested, and that is synonymous with becoming interested in others and, through the many overlapping fields of being, the whole of the planet.

There are many other teachings, although most are derived in some way from the basic precepts discussed above. By its very nature, the Druid Way is organic and those who follow it explore at great length, read widely, think deeply, and act with care. The sources on which they base their teachings and from which they draw their ethical position are often enigmatic. This means that nothing ever becomes rigid for each new contribution to the debate moves things forward in a way that keeps the teachings alive and relevant, firmly rooted in the real world.

5

The Outer World

Although being Druid is a spiritual path it recognizes that the material world is integral to the person and their journey. The world is composed of three elements: the Land, the Sea, and the Sky. Fire is also present, but not regarded as separate. Rather, it is the spirit that inspires the rest of the world (as the sun, for example, or as the flames of the hearth, the heat of the soul, the spark of life, poetic inspiration, and so on). With fire, the house we inhabit becomes a home.

To Druids everything we are is derived from this combination of elements and if we abuse it, either materially or spiritually, we abuse ourselves. If we cut ourselves off from it, we destroy our link to both spiritual and material sustenance.

There are a number of levels to this cosmology that are not easily separated. We can talk of the Land, the Sea, and the Sky as if they were clear-cut and discrete entities, but they each shape the others – physically, spiritually, and symbolically. This is as true today as it has always been, although our largely urban and over-complicated social existence tends to obscure this basic reality.

The Land
Whilst most people would concede that all we have in a material sense is derived from the Land, they would probably stop short of acknowledging that it has a part in shaping our spiritual existence. This is because most people no longer believe that we live in the world. Rather, they believe that we live on it.

Our connection with the Land has been severed. The break occurred when the prevailing metaphysic became one that objectified the world. Druids see this as destructive. They believe it is essential to know the Land – and not just as we learn about it in geography lessons or by studying geology and geomorphology. An emotional relationship must also be forged.

Druids spend a lot of their time exploring the places in which they live, be they rural or urban. They tend to know their local history and are usually involved in their local communities. In bringing the Land alive in this way, they assimilate themselves with it and help stimulate a similar interest in others. And as they become involved with the Land, it helps to shape them and their view of the world. Thus they create an inner landscape that is contiguous, and eventually merges, with the outer landscape.

The inner landscape of the Druid is usually centred on an Inner Grove. It is commonly envisaged as a landscape with which the Druid is familiar and comfortable and contains a specific place where the Druid can form a connection between the outside world and the meditative and ritual work they do within. Here they encounter the very essence of sovereignty.

Understanding the nature of sovereignty is crucial. Sovereignty is the right to rule. It is the right to control. However, this right is not absolute. It is bestowed on those who have earned the right and it comes with many responsibilities. Often portrayed in terms of monarchy, sovereignty is service – service to the Land and to the people. Yet sovereignty also has a personal dimension. The degree to which we can exercise an autonomous existence depends on how well we treat the Goddess and all that she represents. If we follow her precepts our inner and outer landscapes will be green and flowing with clear, sweet water. If we turn our back on the Goddess and abuse her gifts, our landscapes will become a deadly waste and we in turn will wither and die – first in spirit and then in body.

The Sea

The Sea has a symbolic and spiritual quality of a different order.

The Land represents solidity, security, and a sense of belonging – albeit with attendant responsibilities. The Sea has always been seen as something other – vast and fluid. Yet it is not so other that it is wholly beyond our comprehension. For just as it symbolizes the largest and most mysterious of our spiritual concerns, it also symbolizes the smallest and most intimate.

In the case of the largest concern – the cycle of life, death, and rebirth – this is the Sea as personified by the Western Ocean across which Druids believe we all travel when our souls move from this world to the Other.

Ancestral Celts knew, just as we know, that the ocean is but one part of a cycle. Vast as the ocean may be, water also manifests in very small amounts that have a direct effect on our lives. From the ocean, water rises as vapour through the power of the sun. The vapour forms into clouds, which are the fruit of the cycle. They eventually let fall rain or snow. Each drop of rain or flake of snow is a seed that will grow, finally, to become an ocean.

In each drop is to be found the basis for the cycle that Druids use to symbolize and celebrate the self. This is an important teaching of the Druid Way. We lead humble existences, no matter that some may inflate the importance of their own being. We must all eat, drink, excrete, earn a living, keep house, and do all the other day-to-day things that keep body and soul together. And in this, if it is done in accord with truth, is the very basis of spiritual life.

By living simply and acknowledging the true nature of our being, Druids believe that each humble act of life becomes a prayer, part of the conversation between the self and the world. This, of course, can be accentuated with words, as long as they are words said with feeling and with understanding. They must, after all, engage a person with the world and draw them into an ever-closer communion. Mindless repetition of a formula has the opposite effect.

The point of striking up this conversation is to make us pay attention to our actions and to the reasons behind them. This, in turn, helps us to wash away what is superfluous as well as giving us time to see the simpler ways there are of doing things.

And just as the small can be found within the large, so the large can be found within the small. The focus on the relationship of the self with the world inevitably leads to the great mystery of life, death, and rebirth. This is symbolized by the great Sea, which is created by and from those small drops as they flow together in rivulets, streams, and rivers toward the shore where, finally, they feed the ocean.

This cycle is an apt symbol of life. In material form, we think of ourselves as individuals. Yet, for the most part, we are far too integrated with the rest of the world for this to have any absolute meaning. How long does a raindrop remain a raindrop? Even as it falls from the clouds it will collide with others, merge, and reform; just as our personalities are formed and developed by contact with others. Once the raindrop reaches the ground, it enters into a complex of cycles. This experience ineradicably alters the water and all about it and may engage it in many different relationships before it reaches a free-flowing stream and can start on its journey to the sea where identity is lost in the whole. Yet that is not the end. Vapour rises, clouds form, and new raindrops fall to follow a new journey.

The Sky

In many religions, the Sky is seen as the abode of deity. Whilst there are undoubtedly Celtic deities that have strong connection with the Sky, it is by no means an exclusive relationship. They inhabit Land and Sea as well, much as fire does. Indeed, the Celts did not look to the Sky for worship, but for the cycles that regulated the world in which they lived.

Like all people before the invention of mechanical timepieces, ancestral Celts regulated their lives (when necessary) by observing and working with the rhythms created by the movements of the sun and the moon. Although artificial timekeeping and the advent of modern calendars are considered a boon to our modern society, this form of regulation does not fully accord with the way in which our selves relate to the world or attune to our environment. Nor is this simply on the physical level. Druids also attune aspects of their spirituality to the rhythms of the natural world, believing that a basic level of spiritual harmony can be achieved in this way. They also try to allow natural rhythms to guide their everyday lives as far as is possible in a society governed by an artificial standard.

Day and night is the simplest rhythm, breaking life into units that we find easy to cope with. 'Take it a day at a time' is probably advice that goes back many millennia. Following the practice of ancestral Celts, Druids think of each new day as starting just after the sun has set. The setting sun is an obvious, natural marker. It means that all major tasks are undertaken after rest and recuperation and sets a pattern whereby dark and light are not considered opposites or separate entities, but aspects of the same cycle.

Two other major units of time that are important are those governed by the moon. The month, which, as far as we know, was measured from full moon to full moon, was one. The other was the fortnight or fourteen nights (fourteen nights from a given time being half a month). This lunar reckoning was the major calendar for the Celts, and is redolent with symbolism. It was also tied in with the solar cycle, adjustments being made every few years (with a naturally occurring extra moon), and with a recognition of the coincidence of the lunar and solar cycles every nineteen years.

For all their variations, these cycles provide a strong underlying order, originating as they do in the realm that is least accessible to the meddling ambitions and hands of people. The order cannot be altered. The basic rules of life are derived from this natural order – which is why Druids consider many of their teachings to be derived from the world. Yet this realm, the Sky, is also the least rigid for it is the realm of air and the wind.

The air, as represented by the Sky, has important symbolic qualities for the Druid. As living, breathing creatures, our distinct material existence is defined by air. Our very first autonomous act in this world is to inhale; our last is to exhale. The movement of air keeps the fire of life present within us. As we take in air, it follows a journey much like the spiritual journey of the Druid. Inward, first, it traverses the labyrinth until it reaches the very heart of our being. There, in the darkness, it is transformed before being exhaled in new form to contribute to the world.

This is by no means all that is important about, or symbolized by, the tripartite arrangement of this world. These and many more ideas are studied, as are the relationships between the three, component parts of the three, and the inspiring fire that animates them all. Moreover, as with many other aspects of the Druid Way, these are not to be seen as delimiting superstitions. They are tools used to aid in a better understanding of the world, an understanding that does not rely solely on the narrow perspective of analytical empiricism.

6

The Otherworld

The journey of the soul

The final voyage of this life is across the ocean in the West, following the setting sun. However, it is not a voyage of shadows fading into eternal darkness. Death is not an end, merely a changing of place. Beyond the dark, beyond the well-earned sleep, there is light and a new sunrise. Reborn in the Otherworld, we begin the reciprocal to this life and balance out our time here with a life in which the spirit is predominant and readily accepted. There we work toward an understanding of and balance with the material.

Although the Otherworld is often considered a land of summer stars; it is also, when compared with the shadow world in which we live, one of bright daylight. As with much else, it is a matter of perspective. And although the denizens of each world may find the other world perplexing, there is no doubt that the two worlds are inextricably linked – the common medium being ourselves and all other living beings that make the journey between the two.

Connected with the notion of personal responsibility and the immortality of the soul is the belief that we travel together. That is, we are reborn amongst the same people. Our relationships may be different, but our responsibilities remain. Some have taken this to be an indication that both ancestral Celts and modern Druids believe in a form of karma. This is not so.

Responsibility for one's actions lies with the self in the here and now and is an inherent quality of those actions. You do something and you take responsibility for it because it is right to do so, not because there is a reward of some description, be that heaven, a better life, or nirvana. Nor is anything done, or refrained from, because of the threat of punishment, whether damnation and torture in hell, or returning as a 'lesser' life form. Celts did not consider animals to be lesser life forms. They have spirit and are our equals. Many of them are teachers; all of them are guides.

An understanding of the balance between the material and spiritual can be seen in the ancestral Celtic custom of burying personal belongings along with the bodies of those that owned them. This is often taken to be a primitive expression of the belief that you can take it with you. In a sense this is true, but not in the crude way that is often implied. Personal items such as jewellery, weapons, professional tools, games, and the like, all become endowed with the spirit of their owner through prolonged use and close personal contact. They are an integral part of who that person is. This is especially so of any item that is used in ritual. That is why Druids ask for their ceremonial equipment to be buried or cremated with them.

The same is true for relationships. We are shaped in large part by those people, animals, and landscapes with which we have close and prolonged contact. This works for our spirit and for our spiritual understanding as well. To move to the Otherworld (or back to this) without that wider spiritual endowment is to be reborn incomplete, is to be held back on our new journey.

Reverence for our ancestors (and the ability to communicate with them) becomes a great deal easier to understand in the light of this spiritual legacy. If we travel on a number of cycles between this world and the Other, then we are our ancestors.

The search for past life experiences, however, is not much encouraged within Druid tradition, although there are individuals who take an interest. To spend time on lives we have already lived and can do nothing about is considered a waste of this life; as is an undue emphasis on living in the shadow of how we might influence the next life. Understanding the past and having a care for the future are essential elements of right living, but that living should be in the now.

Other worlds

The Otherworld is the place to which souls migrate when our bodies die, the place where they enjoy new lives, and from whence they come that we may be reborn once more in this world. The Otherworld is not a land of the dead. It is not heaven or hell. It is not a supernatural realm at all. These concepts are alien to the Celtic metaphysic. Such definitions have come about as the result of attempting to understand the Celtic view of the world by comparing it with, and using the terminology of, the metaphysic of other peoples and of other times. Both worlds are natural. Both are worlds of the living. They are contiguous one with another and, in places, they overlap.

The cycle that takes us from world to world by means of a series of rebirths is the normal way to make the journey. However, it is not the only way, as many ancient tales will attest. The denizens of one world can visit other worlds and then, with care and luck, return to their own. Such an undertaking is extremely hazardous, not least because it is all too easy to mistake the Otherworld for Faerie or one of the many other worlds.

There is an ancient tradition of voyaging across the Western Sea in search of these other lands. The *imram*, as it is called, is a quest in which whatever is sought is attained not just through physical prowess and endurance, but also through wisdom and a testing of the soul. Such was the power of these early tales that they were adopted into the Christian tradition both as *imrama* and in much altered form as the Grail quest. Other worlds could also be reached through gateways on land, not all of them obvious. There are many tales of people crossing from one world to another without realizing until it is too late.

Arthur made such a journey with a number of heroic

companions. Of all those who went (three shiploads) only seven returned and even then it is not entirely certain that they gained the prize they sought.

The Otherworld is not our natural realm when we are incarnate in this world. Moreover, Faerie is not our natural realm whether we are incarnate in this world or the Other. To travel, or even to attempt to travel, to these places puts us in great danger. Caution and experience can assist us, but even then, they are not absolute guarantees of our safety.

We no longer live in a world that is so accepting of such experience. Scientific materialism has come to dominate thinking and institutions. Talk of, belief in or, worse still, a statement of knowledge about a place like the Otherworld or Faerie, is not taken seriously. Yet the personal experience of those who are open to the whole of reality (rather than the small portion that concerns materialists) is that they are real places and that their denizens are as interested in us as we are in them.

The Otherworld is a place of balance, countering the world that we currently inhabit. Our lives in the Otherworld are lived in spirit and when there, our life's task is to come to understand the material side of our existence so that we may better cope with it when we are incarnate in this world. The mirror of this is true when we are here, for now our life's work is to understand better our spiritual side so that when we move to the Otherworld we can concentrate on understanding our material being. And in both worlds, we are meant to strive for order and for balance.

Many people fear death, yet there is no need. The material body dies, and that process can be uncertain. We lose control and lose our dignity, there is often pain. We all face it and fear of these things is understandable. They are inevitable aspects of the decay of the material body. Yet death itself, the moving on of the soul, is merely the start of a new journey. It is the sunset, with the promise of a new day inherent in the demise of the old.

It is why Druids celebrate a death as the beginning of a new life. They certainly mourn for the loss of a loved one. It is painful for any of us to see someone we love suffer; it is painful coping with the wound caused by their amputation from our lives. When Druids lose loved ones in this world, they remember them, give thanks for having had the chance to share time with them, and celebrate their existence. And one of the best ways of doing that, they believe, is to move on. The lives of the departed can be celebrated each Samhain and, ultimately, all souls will be reunited.

Working with our ancestors should not be confused with travelling to the Otherworld. When Druids consult with their ancestors, it is done with their consent at times when, and in places where, the worlds are coexistent, most notably at Samhain. Many people talk to their dear ones at their grave. It does not mean they believe that person is there, but it is a ritual that enables them to open themselves up and continue the conversations they had when both were still in this world.

This aspect of connection with the Otherworld is harmless and, in some degree, to be encouraged, as long as it does not become obsessive. Keeping open the dialogue we had helps to keep alive the memory of those people as well as allowing us to tap into their wisdom. 'What would Granny have done?' is a more potent question than many imagine – especially if everyone knew Granny well. Her wisdom continues to live in her offspring and she is quite capable of adding to that through them. She has not incarnated in the Otherworld as anyone's Granny, but her soul continues and is well aware of its responsibilities and obligations to the family and to the tribe, even when the concept of tribe has become lost within the other social constructs of our time.

The great voyage that all of us will make (and which Druids believe we have already made on many occasions) is of great importance to us. So, too, is our connection with our ancestors. But our hunger for an understanding of what is to come and of the places to which we will eventually travel does not, and is not allowed to, divert the Druid from their real work, or from the place in which that work is to be done – the here and the now. Sunsets may be spectacular and linger in our memory, but they only last for a tiny fraction of the day. Moreover, if we spend all our time waiting in anticipation of them, the rest of the day is wasted. Treasure each moment. When the sun does finally touch the western horizon, your joy of it will be all the greater for knowing that it is the glory that crowns a day well spent.

Part III

7

The Organization of the Druid Way

How people become Druid

There is no single organization that embraces or represents all Druids. It will come as no surprise, therefore, that there is no single hierarchy or overarching authority. There are no true Archdruids, elected by national assemblies and having responsibility for all Druids in a given region. There are no sets of rules or codes of conduct drawn up by a central authority to be imposed on all who wish to be called Druid. There are no doctrinal courts. Some of the larger Orders do have formal hierarchies, constitutions, and the like, but these are mostly administrative. Many other groups deliberately avoid such structures, and where individuals do have titles, they are explicitly neutral. It follows that there is no officially agreed syllabus of teachings, no accepted single form of ritual, and no universally recognized form of initiation.

Despite all this, Druids do follow a common path with common goals. There are many variations and different approaches, but they are all in the one Forest, and are all searching for Light. They often do this in groups, helping each other along and teaching others about what they have discovered. Authority, where it is recognized, derives from experience and wisdom.

This situation exists because material and spiritual autonomy of the person is central to the Druid Way. For this reason, Druids do not preach to others with the intention of converting them. The very idea is anathema. Druids *will* teach and they do explain what they believe if they are asked. However, one of the early spiritual lessons they teach is that every person must make the journey for themselves.

The notion of autonomy applies particularly to children and young people. Whilst Druids will bring up their own children in the spirit of their beliefs, they will not impose them on their offspring. In ancestral times, the Age of Choice (at which a person was deemed old enough to be responsible for their decisions and actions) was fourteen. Whilst some children these days may be mature enough to decide on a spiritual path at that age, Druids will rarely accept people into an Order or Grove on a formal basis until they are eighteen. This does not mean that Druids will not teach about their beliefs to people who are younger, but they believe everyone should make their own choice about their spiritual path, and only once they are mature enough to take this step.

Given all this, it is legitimate to ask how people become Druid. Most Druids have actually been Druid for some time before they put a name to it. They generally start alone, finding themselves attracted to Celtic literature and history, and leading lives that are closely in accord with the Celtic metaphysic. Many are happy to continue in this way and feel no need to become involved with others. A significant number, however, decide that it would be good to share this interest and growing awareness, learning from those further along the path.

There are many ways in which this can occur. Local groups and moots (open pagan meetings) may advertise, friends may know people, and very often chance events will open up contacts at the right time. In whatever way the path first attracts people, they will invariably encounter some of the larger groups and Orders. They may decide to join or be invited into a Grove. For some, this is just a phase and they move on after a few years to explore the path in their own way. For others it is exactly what they want and they immerse themselves in the new group of like-minded people.

Druid Orders

Originally, Druids were just Druids and integral to Celtic Society. The Druid Orders are a 'modern' invention of the Revivalists of the eighteenth century. Some Orders are very small, much like extended families, and have grown out of the common experience and shared ideas of members in a relatively small location. Others have thousands of members worldwide and necessarily work to a different dynamic.

Most Druid Orders have a hierarchy of people responsible for the running of the organization. There will often be a Chief Druid in overall charge, with others in positions of responsibility within the Order. These positions vary, but revivalist Druid titles such as Pendragon and Scribe may be used. The senior members usually form a Council that discusses the running of the Order on a regular basis. Members belong either directly to the Order or to Groves within the Order (the latter if the Order covers a wide geographical area).

A number of Orders offer correspondence courses on Druidic teachings to which people can subscribe. Indeed, with some Orders, you may not be considered a member unless you are prepared to study the course. The quality and content of these courses varies and often reflects the particular interests and perspective of the hierarchy. Some are very much influenced by the eighteenth-century Revivalism whilst others eschew this material entirely and work from Celtic literary and folk sources as well as historical and archaeological material. Some Orders also organize lectures, workshops, and camps, where more focused forms of learning can take place.

The organization of most Orders, and the construction of their courses, is tripartite. The three divisions are usually called grades, one each for Bard, Vate (also known as Ovate), and Druid. This is another invention of the eighteenth-century Revivalists, based on their interpretation of classical sources. Those Orders and groups that use the grade system tend to be the ones that have the most rigid hierarchies. Most Druids regard the threefold division as a useful means of understanding, treating the three divisions as being akin to interwoven branches or paths.

In learning to become Druid in the present day, people explore all three branches. Bardic studies come first as they are the ones best suited to unlocking the mind's potential to understand the world in a new way – essential if one is to understand and adopt the Celtic metaphysic. Through an emphasis on the arts (in the broadest sense of that term), people learn to see things as connected and as unified. They also learn to see things intuitively and to value that form of cognition as being as important as any other.

They are then ready to handle studying those areas that are associated with the Vate. Where Bardic studies involve the senses and a study of the outer, communal, material world, Vatic studies concentrate on the inner, spiritual journey, the mysteries of life and death.

Having made the journey inwards to the very heart of what it means to be Druid, having faced themselves, having become familiar with the many other worlds and levels and layers of existence of which they are a part, and having become attuned with them, a Druid is then ready to return to the world and guide others on the Way. Any Druid will tell you that once they begin teaching others, they also go back to basics and start again on a new cycle of learning. In this way, they bring an entirely new perspective to their connection with, and understanding of, the world. They are able to refine what they know and understand, coming that bit closer to wisdom.

Groves

A Grove is a working community of Druids. They provide companionship, an opportunity for like-minded people to work and explore together, and a much more immediate sense of belonging than is sometimes afforded by an Order. There are many such Groves and groups. Most not only celebrate the cycle of the year but also organize other activities such as camps, retreats, initiations, and social events.

Groves can be part of the main structure of, or affiliated to, an Order. Equally, they can be independent of any other grouping. If a Grove is part of an Order, members will need to belong to the Order before they can be invited to become part of the Grove. Some Orders have Grade Groves, which means that the Druid Grove can only be attended by those in the Druid Grade; Vate or Ovate Groves welcome both Ovates and Druids, whilst all grades can attend a Bardic Grove.

A Grove can be as small as two people in which case, it rarely maintains the formality of a larger group. There is no upper limit on numbers although, as with any collection of people, group dynamics dictate against too large a gathering being successful. When a Grove reaches a certain size it may split into sister Groves, which function separately for formal rituals and teaching, but come together for informal celebrations. How the Groves are organized internally is very much up to the members (although some Orders insist on certain formalities). It is normal for the most experienced Druid or Druids to preside over ritual and be responsible for any teaching that takes place.

Closed Groves

Some independent Groves are known as Closed Groves. There is nothing different about them other than the fact that entry is strictly by invitation only. Such Groves usually come about as the result of a group of people who are already friends deciding to work together spiritually. Most members use the forum of the Grove for formal occasions, ritual, and for group teaching whilst working on their own to explore particular interests in, and aspects of, the Druid Way.

The notion can seem both patronizing and elitist, as well as having overtones of secret societies and cults. A Closed Grove, however, will exist simply so that members can preserve something that works for them, not least their close friendships.

Lone or Hedge Druids

A Hedge Druid is one who works substantially alone. There are probably more Hedge Druids than there are Druids in the Orders. This is not surprising. There is, after all, a streak of anarchism in the Druid Way that derives from the fundamental belief that each person is responsible for their own thoughts and actions – something that cannot be fully realized within a hierarchy.

There are, of course, other reasons why people work alone. They may not know any other Druids, or their personal circumstances may make it difficult to meet with others. Some do not wish to practice openly for fear of persecution – a reality, even today. On a more positive note, many Druids simply feel that working alone is the best way for them to explore the Forest.

There is a long and venerable history of lone working. The majority of Druids in ancestral times, once they had completed their training, would have been attached to something like a ditched enclosure, a sacred site, a tribal leader, or even a village – offering their wisdom and practical skills to all who were in need of them.

Hedge Druids fulfil an extremely important role within the tradition and are by no means any less Druid for not working within a Grove or an Order. They tend to focus on their own exploration and concentrate on their own practices without having to do what others ordain. They do not need to become involved with group politics and can do things how they like and when they like, following their own path and adding to the great commonwealth of knowledge and understanding as they go.

Of course, there is a down side. It is always good for a person to be part of a community of like-minded souls. It is here that they can discuss things and pass on what they have learned, as well as gain emotional and spiritual strength from knowing they are not alone. Moreover, it takes considerable strength of will to carry on when there is a lack of connection with the wider Druid community – a particular problem at the festivals. That is why most Hedge Druids maintain contact with other Druids, usually people with whom they have become close friends.

8

Ceremonial and Ritual Practice

The life of a Druid is informed by the rhythms of the Land, the Sea, and the Sky. They celebrate this with an annual round of ceremonies. Some are relatively fixed events, working with the dance of sun, moon, and stars. These are Imbolc, spring equinox (Alban Eiler), Beltane, summer solstice (Alban Hefin), Lughnasad, autumn equinox (Alban Elfed), Samhain, and winter solstice (Alban Arthan) – collectively referred to as the eightfold year. Others are more intimate rituals, marking the major events of their lives or accompanying the daily and mundane activities that Druids undertake.

There is, of course, a great deal more to being Druid than performing rituals. However, the act of celebration through ritual is one of the major means by which Druids integrate the material and spiritual aspects of their lives.

All ritual takes place within a circle. The physical shape in the material world, even if it is drawn in the air or the mind, is a powerful presence. What is more, in keeping with all that Druids hold sacred, it is temporary. The circle is always closed at the finish and the physical place of ritual is left as if no one had been there.

The creation of this space is a first and simple step in using the material to bring thought and action to bear on the spiritual. However, Druids do not use one to gain enhanced engagement with the other. Rather, they work within the space they have created to move onward, using the aspect of their being in which they are deeply seated (the material) to secure their integration with that aspect of their being to which they strongly aspire (the spiritual).

The shape of the ritual within the circle is also important to Druids. The objects used, the words spoken, and the physical actions – all act as triggers. Their cumulative effect is profound as they become imbued with universal and personal symbolic significance.

The more a given ritual is enacted, the more a Druid is able to concentrate on content and meaning rather than form. This creates a journey through the years from formal expression and the material into the underlying principles on which these are based. Performing ritual on a regular basis, therefore, is a long-term form of meditation.

Meditation is not used by Druids to try to attain a state of disconnectedness. Rather, they focus on particular symbols and myth cycles, as well as deities and entities, in order to reach a deeper understanding of, and more profound connection with, the worlds they inhabit.

Ceremony need not be a matter of gravity and pomp – robes, paraphernalia, obscure rites, and archaic language. It can be enacted simply and alone or in small groups, and it is often more appropriate to do so. Large formal events have their place, but just as people cannot always live on a mystical high, so Druids cannot always approach their veneration of the worlds in a formal way. They learn, rather, to touch and appreciate all the worlds in an intimate fashion.

This more intimate approach is often accomplished through prayer. Prayer is the daily conversation a Druid has with the sacred. It is the way in which Druids attune themselves to the everyday, for it is in the everyday that Druids believe true magic is to be found – in such things as the growing of food, cooking, companionship, and all the other basic sights, sounds, and experiences of our lives.

There are two sides to the conversation. Whilst we are all very good at talking, when it comes to listening many of us have closed ears. One of the things that Druids learn very early is how to open their ears to the other side of the conversation and listen to what the world has to tell them. Druids are not made by reading books (although books certainly help in the absence of Druid colleges and mentors). Druids are made by learning to see (rather than just look) and learning to listen (rather than just hear). They are made by engaging with the world and with the sacred.

The eightfold year (Wheel of the year)

Of all the rituals associated with Druids in the popular imagination, it is those that mark out the turning of the year that first come to mind. These festivals are celebrated every six weeks or so. In terms of ancestral practice, there is a degree of controversy over the eightfold year. Four of the festivals are well attested and have even survived to the present day in popular form, celebrated in various Celtic countries and regions. These are Imbolc, Beltane, Lughnasad, and Samhain. They delineate the seasons and celebrate the agricultural cycle.

The solar festivals mark the equinoxes and solstices. In all likelihood, they were quiet, formal occasions creating a mystical atmosphere in which people could reflect on and give thanks for their relationship with the spiritual domain. Some scholars dispute that the solar festivals existed. However, given the number of solar deities in the Celtic pantheon and the fact that the dates of the solar festivals were appropriated by the Christian Church, it seems likely they were, in fact, extremely important to ancestral Celtic peoples.

The solar festivals are absolute within the year, since those four days define it in astronomical terms (even if the Gregorian calendar moves a day or two back and forth about them). The lunar festivals fall approximately forty-five days after solar festivals. Given the complexities of modern life, most present-day Druids celebrate the eightfold year on conventional dates (and very often on the weekend nearest those). Others perform quiet private rituals at the correct time and more open ceremonies at the nearest convenient date. They believe that an understanding of the cycle and the keeping of it in spirit is much more important and effective than soulless pedantry.

Rites of passage

Rites of passage follow the same cycle of birth, growth, maturity, death, and rebirth that is to be found in the ceremonies of the eightfold year, but the emphasis is different and the focus is much narrower.

Druid rituals, as Druids are the first to admit, are not ancient. No one knows how ancestral Celts made formal celebration of the major events of their lives. We do not even know for certain which events they considered important. However, from a study of law texts and other sources more prosaic than the myths and legends, it is possible to derive a list of eight important events that modern Druids believe should be marked by ceremony and, where appropriate, by celebration. These are: birth, naming, the age of choice, independence, binding, unbinding, death, and interment. This is by no means an exhaustive list of such rites – the nature of what is celebrated prompts many Druids to add others that are personally significant.

Because they are personal, relating to the self and to immediate family and friends, the shape and texture of these rituals are different from those of the eightfold year. Most of the rites are marked by the kind of informality one expects of close relationships, for the focus is on people and the family rather than on deity. Even with solemn occasions such as marriage and burial where a degree of formality is appropriate, the emphasis is always on the personal.

Taken together, these rituals are seen as the circle of life. They are an integral part of the material and spiritual existence in which Druids celebrate their selves. This is not egotistical. Rather, it is an acknowledgment of their personal being in a way that links them with the universe, nurtures their spirit, and brings balance into their everyday lives.

This is all too often ignored by those who seek a spiritual path. Their whole focus is on mystical experience, on the glamour of the big ritual. Druids are certainly aware of the larger picture, but they do not believe they can successfully explore that larger domain unless they have an understanding of their own being in its normal, everyday existence.

The personal

The eightfold year is a ritual manifestation of the Sky and is concerned with the world. Rites of passage relate to the Land and are concerned with community. The final set of rites discussed here is concerned with the personal and connect with the Sea. We have already seen how the Sea relates to the largest of our personal spiritual concerns, the journey of the soul to the Otherworld. Here, the concern is with the spiritual in the everyday world and how the self deals with its immediate experience of the world in which we all live. This is achieved through prayer.

Such a conversation is the means by which a Druid constantly explores and renews their relationship with the world. Through the ages, Celts have had a prayer and a blessing for every conceivable occasion. Where they lacked one their nature was such that they could easily extemporize. With short rhymes and lengthy pieces, they invoked the goddesses, gods, and spirits to weave together the everyday world with the world of the spirit.

Meditation

Meditation is an essential part of any spiritual path and has been practiced worldwide for at least three thousand years. Some people believe that meditation is primarily an Eastern discipline. There is, however, a long and well-established tradition of meditation within pre-Christian Celtic religious and spiritual practice.

Druids do not meditate in order to transcend this world. They seek clearer states of consciousness in order to become better integrated with it. Becoming absorbed by the sunset colours across the sky, feeling the grass with bare feet after a shower of rain, holding a peach-coloured shell, or sitting on a windy hilltop simply to experience the wind, are all states of meditation best described in the later poems attributed to Taliesin. Although a clear and settled mind is necessary for this, the belief that all meditation is done in an uncomfortable full-lotus yoga position whilst trying to empty the mind of thought and emotion is unfounded.

Meditation is often referred to as visualization or pathworking. In visualization, images are chosen (be they imagined or observed in the world) for their symbolic or elemental quality in order to allow the Druid to analyze and synthesize their relationship with this aspect of the world. This kind of meditation is usually done alone. With pathworking, paths or journeys are constructed (usually from Celtic mythology) to introduce Druids to narrative forms, to deities, and to ideas. These are often used as teaching tools and a Druid will narrate the journey whilst others listen and explore the images they are given. Pathworking is especially useful with those who are new to the Druid Way as an experienced practitioner can guide them safely through the journey and back to where they started. Insightful discussions often follow such sessions.

There is one other type of visualization technique – the Inner Grove. This is, in effect, an inner sanctuary that all Druids have. The nature of the sanctuary varies with each Druid. However, it is a place of rest, a calm centre in a hectic world, a spiritual hearth where Druids can centre themselves. From this place, they can make journeys into the deeper reaches of the Forest in the knowledge that there is somewhere secure to which they can return.

Many people dismiss as mere imagination the notion of other dimensions to our life. But there are many ways of understanding the world. One way is imagination, a faculty that should not be dismissed as mere make-believe. It is much more than that. Imagination is the ability to experience the world other than by our five senses; it is the ability to experience aspects of the world we would not normally be able to encounter. Without imagination, a Druid will say, we cannot have compassion. Without imagination, we cannot transcend our material existence.

9

Being Druid in the World

Being Druid is not just about ceremonial and ritual practice. It is an entire way of life, expressed in everything that a Druid does. This is because becoming Druid involves adopting a new outlook on the world. For many, the change is gradual and, in itself, does not cause problems. However, living true to the Druid Way can be difficult.

Pagans in general and Druids in particular face prejudice for their beliefs and practices. In the extreme, this has involved people losing their jobs, having their children taken away by social service departments, and more vulnerable members of the pagan community being driven to suicide. It is ignorance of the Druid Way, however, rather than outright prejudice that is the main problem encountered by Druids when dealing with the rest of the world.

The popular image of Druids is derived from highly distorted media portrayals, along with passing reference to the Druid Way in works of fiction where it is used to add a hint of exoticism and menace. It is no wonder that when Druids feel it necessary to let others know what path they follow, they are met with confusion. Few Druids, therefore, go out of their way to announce their beliefs to the outside world. The Druid Way is a quiet and private relationship.

For all that these problems do occur, they are atypical. The major problem faced by Druids is how they organize their ordinary everyday lives in a world where the prevailing metaphysic is at odds with their own. All Druids, of course, are different, but on the whole they aim for simplicity. The notion of simplicity is related to the Celtic metaphysic and may best be described as the practical application of the Celtic vision of the world to everyday life.

Simplicity is the art of finding the least complicated route. Living simply is a complex matter, a reflection of the complexity of the world. Where life is involved, the natural order of things is toward increasingly complex systems. Yet no matter how complex, it is all necessary. Human endeavour has taken what is complex and elegant and complicated it for no obvious good reason.

When things become complicated, they all too easily obscure what is needful. This is true at all levels, from the most basic of material requirements to the highest of spiritual aspirations. In order to support the complicated structures that are erected, people behave mendaciously, create problems that did not previously exist and waste resources solving them, avoid or ignore the problems that do exist, destroy life, and promulgate war. Indeed, violence and war are supreme expressions of the complications upon which modern society is built.

Simplicity shuns what is complicated. It is a search for the complex, a search for the most natural way in which to express one's self and conduct the mundane activities of one's life. It means learning to see through the complications of society so that we manage our lives in ways that sidestep those entanglements.

There are those who would call this opting out. In a sense, this is true. It is opting out of a system that Druids see as materialistic, violent, and destructive; a system that has abjured the truth and has no moral basis. Druids try to minimize their support of such an arrangement. In the first instance, this involves looking at every aspect of how they live their day-to-day lives and embracing that which is simple. Simplicity, however, requires trust and it requires honour. Much of what is complicated about modern society derives from a system based on a lack of trust – not just between individuals, but also in the world about us. The more complicated society becomes, the easier it is for people to exploit any trust that does exist and to foster doubt in what is merely complex.

Trust is an expression of truth. Druids believe that we each need to assess our lives to remove all the complicated clutter that has built up around us like a dead weight. This is not simply a matter of ridding ourselves of all those material things we do not actually need. Every part of life should come under scrutiny so that our whole approach is simplified and attuned to the way in which the world works. To do this, it is necessary to trust in the Land, trust in the Sea, and trust in the Sky; trust that these can and will provide for all the genuine needs of humankind.

Simplicity is, of course, relative. There are no absolutes, not least because each person has their own relationship with the world. It is not possible to make hard and fast rules about what is simple, because such rules would run counter to the Celtic metaphysic. They would complicate matters.

For Druids, balance is the key and that, they believe, begins within each of us. Whether we like it or not, we are all part of the material world. If we are fortunate, we have jobs, buy food, wear clothes, have a roof over our heads, and have leisure time. Unfortunately, many people are caught up in this side of life. They become so unbalanced by the merry-go-round of material existence that all other forms of thought and action are considered strictly out-of-bounds.

The Druid Way is a spiritual path that accepts that we have a material existence, accepts that the material is essential to our wellbeing. It is not a path of deprivation where one must give up all possessions and become parasitic on others in order to find personal salvation. Indeed, it is not even a path of personal salvation. The Druid Way is a path of balance between, and integration of, the material and the spiritual in order to effect healing. Failure to integrate the material and the spiritual means they cannot be kept in balance. Without balance, we end up with extremism. Go too far down the material road and the spirit withers, along with compassion and love. Go too far or too obsessively with the spiritual and we deny our material nature.

Acknowledging the relative nature of simplicity, the need for integration and balance, means placing trust in our intuitive faculties. This is not easy. We are taught from a very early age that there is something not quite right about doing that. But this scepticism is because purely rational and analytical minds have insufficient tools with which to distinguish between intuitive decision-making and a purely egotistical and emotional response to one's surroundings.

Each decision about life has to be taken on its merits. It has to be done openly with complete acceptance of one's responsibility for what one does, says, and thinks. Taking such responsibility is another aspect of simplicity that many find difficult to accommodate. Although we do not have absolute control over our lives (for even simple lives are complex and involve other people, as well as social, economic, and natural environments), acting responsibly and in full knowledge of what we do and what effect that has is part and parcel of what we are as self-aware beings. We cannot claim self-awareness as part of what makes us human and then turn our backs on what that implies.

Inherent in the idea of simplicity is the Druid's rejection of conventional ideas of 'progress'. This is a term that is invariably used to mean increased material complication and it rarely coincides with any true improvement in our lives – materially or spiritually. It is also tied inexorably to a linear view of the world, which polarizes all things. Yet for the Druid, the world is cyclical. Improvement in our lives, therefore, is achieved by lessening the complications and realizing that each point on the cycle (just as each time of the day and each season of the year) will provide for what is needed.

Rejection of conventional ideas of progress and the linear allows the Druid to forge a different relationship with time.

Many of the complications in our lives and in the world as a whole come from the distorted vision we have of this dimension. A simple life is based in the now. That does not mean it has no regard for the past or the future. Indeed, those who live simply pay more heed to those things than do those who live linear lives. However, those who live in linear fashion are always trying to live their lives in the future and it cannot be done.

Simplicity is also an acknowledgment that we cannot control the natural world. Accepting that is another aspect of the trust that is required. Stepping back from the notion of control also means accepting that humans are not superior beings with an innate right to do as they wish with the planet and its inhabitants. Druids believe that we do not and cannot own the world any more than we can control it. We have a place in the world, and our particular form of intelligence may have a role in its preservation. We may even be arrogant enough to call ourselves stewards provided we are genuinely prepared to accept the responsibilities of such a position. However, we are no more than stewards and never can be.

To find their place in the world, Druids will act appropriately. In the things they do and the things they make, they try for the minimum level of refinement. Materials that they use are as close to natural as possible and are biodegradable or, at the least, recyclable. Their actions accord with systems that use least energy most efficiently, that do not waste materials, and that do not tie them up in meaningless activity.

All of this requires that Druids become aware of the true cost of things. Not just the price on the ticket stuck to the box, but the social and environmental costs of production, as well as the miles travelled between sourcing raw material, getting the finished product into their homes, and disposing of all the waste material the product produces. This also applies to their relationships and all the other non-material aspects of their lives. They look at them all carefully and find that there are invariably simpler, truer, and less destructive ways of doing things.

It is obvious that there is a high degree of ambiguity and paradox within the notion of simplicity being found by embracing the complex. Ambiguity and paradox, however, are part of the world. They belong in life and are great teachers for they provide a timeless means by which to explore the mysteries of the world and human existence within it. To embrace simplicity, as Druids embrace it, is to embrace the complexity of the world, accepting that such complexity is not in any way alien. Indeed, it is a declaration that in their everyday lives, in their thoughts and actions, in their whole being, in the material and the spiritual, they are a part of the whole.

Further Reading

The list that follows is not, by any stretch of the imagination, a definitive one. There are thousands of books in print on the Celts, their beliefs, the Druids and the modern Druid Way. I have tried to provide here a list of books that will allow you to take the next step in exploring this fascinating subject. In turn, many of them have bibliographies that will lead you to other works of interest.

Bonewits, I. 2006. *Bonewits's Essential Guide to Druidism*. New York: Citadel Press.

Bradley, I. 1993. *The Celtic Way*. London: Darton, Longman & Todd.

Carr-Gomm, P. 1991. *The Elements of the Druid Tradition*. London: Element Books.

Chadwick, N. 1971. *The Celts*. London: Penguin.

Cunliffe, B. 1997. *The Ancient Celts*. Oxford: Oxford University Press.

Cunliffe, B. 2003. *The Celts - A Very Short Introduction*. Oxford: Oxford University Press.

Darrah, J. 1994. *Paganism in Arthurian Romance*. Woodbridge: Boydell Press.

Dillon, M. and Chadwick, N. 1967. *The Celtic Realms*. London: Weidenfeld and Nicolson.

Ellis, P. B. 1994. *The Druids*. London: Constable.

Ellis, P. B. 1998. *The Ancient World of the Celts*. London: Constable.

Green, M. 1986. *The Gods of the Celts*. Stroud: Sutton.

Greywind. 2001. *the Voice within the Wind*. Girvan: Grey House in the Woods.

Guest, C. [tr] 2000. *The Mabinogion*. London: HarperCollins.

James, S. 1993. *Exploring the World of the Celts*. London: Thames and Hudson.

Jones, L. E. 1998. *Druid Shaman Priest*. Enfield Lock: Hisarlik Press.

Jones, P. and Pennick, N. 1995. *A History of Pagan Europe*. London: Routledge.

Kendrick, T. D. 2003 (1927). *Druids and Druidism*. Mineola: Dover.

Koch, J. T. and Carey, J. [eds] 2003. *The Celtic Heroic Age*. 4th Edition. Aberystwyth: Celtic Studies Publications.

MacCulloch, J. A. 1992 (1911). *The Religion of the Ancient Celts*. London: Constable.

MacKillop, J. 1998. *Dictionary of Celtic Mythology*. Oxford: Oxford University Press.

Matthews, C. 1989. *The Elements of the Celtic Tradition*. London: Element Books.

Ó hÓgáin, D. 1999. *The Sacred Isle - Belief and Religion in Pre-Christian Ireland*. Woodbridge: Boydell.

Orr, E. R. 1998. *Principles of Druidry*. London: Thorsons.

Orr, E. R. 2008. *Living with Honour: A Pagan Ethics*. Winchester: O-Books.

Owen, A. L. 1962. *The Famous Druids*. Oxford: Oxford University Press.

Piggott, S. 1985. *The Druids*. Revised Edition. London: Thames and Hudson.

Rees, A. and Rees, B. 1961. *Celtic Heritage*. London: Thames and Hudson.

Rolleston, T. W. 1986 (1911). *Myths and Legends of the Celtic Race*. London: Constable.

Ross, A. 1992. *Pagan Celtic Britain*. Revised Edition. London: Constable.

Ross, A. 2004. *Druids*. Stroud: Tempus.

Talboys, G. K. 2005. *Way of the Druid*. Winchester: O Books.

White, J. and Talboys, G. K. 2004. *Arianrhod's Dance*. Girvan: Grey House in the Woods.

White, J. and Talboys, G. K. 2005. *the Path through the Forest*. 2nd Edition. Girvan: Grey House in the Woods.

York, M. 2003. *Pagan Theology*. New York: New York University Press.

B O O K S

O is a symbol of the world, of oneness and unity. In different cultures it also means the "eye," symbolizing knowledge and insight. We aim to publish books that are accessible, constructive and that challenge accepted opinion, both that of academia and the "moral majority."

Our books are available in all good English language bookstores worldwide. If you don't see the book on the shelves ask the bookstore to order it for you, quoting the ISBN number and title. Alternatively you can order online (all major online retail sites carry our titles) or contact the distributor in the relevant country, listed on the copyright page.

See our website www.o-books.net for a full list of over 500 titles, growing by 100 a year.

And tune in to myspiritradio.com for our book review radio show, hosted by June-Elleni Laine, where you can listen to the authors discussing their books.

MySpiritRadio